Mom Has A Second Job

Judith Mattison

Mom Has A Second Job

Prayer Thoughts for Working Mothers

AUGSBURG Publishing House • Minneapolis

MOM HAS A SECOND JOB

Copyright © 1980 Augsburg Publishing House

Library of Congress Catalog Card No. 80-65548

International Standard Book No. 0-8066-1793-4

Scripture quotations unless otherwise noted are from
the Revised Standard Version of the Bible, copyright
1946, 1952, and 1971 by the Division of Christian
Education of the National Council of Churches.

MANUFACTURED IN THE UNITED STATES OF AMERICA

Contents

Preface

ALL MOTHERS WORK—bold, capital letters. ALL mothers work. This book is designed for those who also hold a job outside the home.

Some mothers work out of necessity, for family income needs. Some are single parents and feel the total financial burden of a family. Some mothers work because they enjoy a particular job. In any case, a mother has many considerations as she attempts to balance her giving of herself to her family as well as to her job responsibilities. She may have mixed feelings about her choice of working or the job she holds. From time to time she is tired or frustrated. On the other hand, a working mother may experience excitement and stimulation, pride and a sense of family cooperation.

Whatever her situation, a mother needs to know she can lean on someone to help her through the hard times. She needs to share her good moments with someone. She needs to balance her feelings of satisfaction and responsibility, her desire to be a "good" parent with her ability to contribute to a working situation. She can turn to God because he is always present in our lives. We can rely on him to lead us in making wise choices. We can trust that God understands our battles with guilt and frustration. We certainly can be grateful to him for the good times that come to all of us. And we can hope that with God's help we can adjust attitudes and behaviors so that we are good stewards of our time, abilities, and love wherever we find ourselves; at home or at work.

These prayer thoughts may not exactly describe the specific situations in which we find ourselves, but it is hoped they touch some of the experiences which mothers who work outside the home share, or that they stimulate our thinking about our lives as women in a dual role. It is surely a gift to be able to work and to be blessed with children who need nurturing. God help us to do the job in the best way we each know how; as diverse as those ways may be. He will be there to help us if we call. This book is an attempt to begin the conversation with him.

Early Morning Reluctance

Lord,
I can hardly face the morning.
Sometimes when I awaken
I lack the energy I need for the day.
I want to roll over and go back to sleep.
But I've much to do
   breakfasts to prepare
   dressing, organizing
   and off again to work.

I do not greet every day with joy.
It is part of life,
to cling tenaciously to living
yet unthinkingly wish away its demands.
I would do better to stop a moment
and look carefully at the gifts of a new day—
life, breath, health, family.
I could stand quietly outdoors
   read from my Bible
   give someone a hug.
Thank you, Lord, for another day.
May I dedicate it to your service
by using my strengths and gifts
for others.

My Part-Time Job

They say part-time employees
are the most efficient.
They are less likely to waste time
at coffee breaks or long lunches.
They tend to work hard
and leave.

Thanks for this part-time job, Lord.
I like being home with my family
and I also like working outside our home.
I appreciate an economy where
this is possible.
I am stimulated by the people I meet
and I enjoy sharing those experiences
with my family.
I do work hard
  at my job
  and at home
and I enjoy both.
Thank you, Lord.

My Children Are Learning Independence

Today after school my children
  took the bus to the library,
  went to the YMCA to swim,
  and met me after work.
They've become noticeably more independent
since I've gone to work.
They help with meals
and manage well after school.
They have made more decisions
as individuals
and as part of the family.
They aren't afraid of new situations
or unexpected changes in routine.

This growth is one of the
unexpected benefits of my working.
It's good for everyone.
Rather than hovering over them or interfering,
I tend to encourage and set them free.
I'm not so much avoiding my parenting role
as I am being more realistic
about their abilities
and their use of good judgment.
Help me to wisely foster their independence
so they will become mature and confident adults.

Thanks for Good Health

They say mothers haven't time to be sick.
Well, neither have working mothers.
Thanks, Lord, for my good health.

I respect this amazing mechanism—
my body—
more and more as I age.
I function
I eat and drink
and miraculously I grow.
I have strength and intelligence for
  sometimes long days
  heavy work
  concentrated reasoning.
My limbs are flexible,
my hands agile,
my eyes see!
Gratitude wells up inside me as I realize
what a great miracle it is
to live and be healthy.
Thanks, Lord, thanks.

My Work Never Ends

Help!
I need a day off.
I work at my job
    in my kitchen
    in the yard
    in the basement utility room.
I never get time off.
I'm responsible all the time
and I notice the areas where I slip—
    fewer nice dinners
    missing children's sports events
    weeds in the garden
    cobwebs in the den.

Part of working outside the home
is this sense of unending responsibility.
But I may be overreacting today.
I have more help from my family
than I used to have.
My garden isn't perfect,
but it's all right.
My family hardly has time
for big dinners on weekdays anyway.
Now that I think of it,
the cobwebs were there before I
started working outside the home.
And what's wrong with allowing myself

a little free time
to play tennis
or read a book?
It does me good to relax.
I'm sorry, Lord.
I expected too much of myself.
I was trying to be self-sufficient,
all-powerful and perfect, again.
Forgive me.

A Music Lesson

I enjoy going to my child's music lesson.
Whether it's a "winner"
or an average performance,
I get pleasure from hearing it.
This is part of a child's growing—
   learning a skill
   appreciating the art of music.
These lessons are possible
because I'm earning extra income.
It's one of the bonuses
of working outside the home.
With it comes the responsibility
   to encourage his learning
   to be helpful when possible
   to listen to a lesson when I can.
It's not enough to give the child
lessons or opportunities
and fade away into my busy life.
I need to encourage him
listen to him, laugh and applaud,
enjoy the opportunity with him.
That way we're both growing.
Thank you, Lord.
Help me do a good job with this experience.

Cooperative Parenting

Thanks, Lord, for other parents who help.
I need them.
It's a relief to know that my neighbor
will welcome my boy if he locks himself out.
I appreciate my friend
who cares for my daughter when she's sick.
Thanks for the women and men who
    do the driving for field trips
    lead the Cub Scouts
    help the teacher
    organize a confirmation retreat.
Although I also help,
I am grateful for those people
who offer their time
to benefit my children.
I will not take advantage of them, Lord.
I will not slough off my responsibilities on them.
But I do appreciate their interest
and concern for all our families.
Help me find and remember ways to thank them.
We live in a cooperative world—
you intended it to be so.
Help me to do my part
and to thank others for their help.

Guilt Feelings

I feel guilty.
Perhaps going to work is a selfish thing to do.
Perhaps my children need me
in the morning, after school.
I am often rushed—do I listen enough?

Teach me, Lord,
to weigh my situation honestly.
Help me to know the difference
between being supportive of them
and overprotective.
Help me trust their capabilities
without shrinking from my responsibilities
or losing opportunities to love.
Give me strength to do well
at work and at home.
Forgive my mistakes.

Guilt is counterproductive.
I can make good decisions
whether I work outside the home or not.
I can accept your forgiveness
    make amends
    change my course when necessary
and continue to improve
without guilt.

Getting Organized

I've always been a list-maker, Lord.
And I've been fairly efficient most of the time.
But when I wasn't working outside our home
it was easy to let things slide.
I could always "do it tomorrow."
And when I was home,
I'd forget I'd washed a load of clothes
until I happened to go back to the laundry room
four hours later.
I was easily distracted from one task to another.
It drove me crazy.
Now I've had to reorganize my style.
I plan ahead and attempt only those things
which are very important or within my capabilities.
I don't move furniture on a whim
and I leave the closet emptying until
I need to get it done.
I am more organized.
I know it is because I'm working
that I have been more careful and organized.
I see it as a good change.
My children tend to imitate my behavior
and I tend to put out fewer fires
in a state of hysteria.
I don't waste time wishing
or thinking about the fact
that I can "do it tomorrow."
Actually, I think I have more time,
if I want to claim it,
for things which are important to me.
This is a little bonus.
Thank you, Lord.

Leave a Little Dust

When my friend had twins she about went crazy
until her husband encouraged her to relax—
to let some things go.
Well, I have twins too—
twin jobs—
and I need to let go or I'll be sick.

Send your kind Spirit, Lord,
to help me reassess myself
and my expectations.
I'm trying to do too much
and I lack the confidence
   to say no
   to quit an activity
   to not work extra hours
   to have a less-than-perfect household.

You don't expect perfection, Lord—
only that I be a good steward
of my time and abilities.
Perhaps I should listen more to the children
or reread my devotional
and leave a little dust.

Saturday Expectations

Sometimes I hate Saturdays.
I have such high expectations for them—
    cleaning
    straightening
    errands
    a full agenda.
But my idea of Saturday
clashes with my family's expectations—
    sleeping late
    leisurely breakfast
    playing outdoors
    visiting friends.
We bicker and complain
and run into each other,
unaccustomed to having everyone home.
There is no organized structure
and we all feel frustrated
by the expectations of others.

Help us, Lord,
to find ways to talk over
our individual hopes for Saturday
and reach a consensus
which is acceptable to all.
Help us hear each other.
And let us not be so discouraged by
    the inconveniences
    the frustrations
    the interpersonal collisions of family life
that we give up on our desire
to be a caring, understanding family.
We can work things out with your help.

Consumers

There are moments when I see it clearly.
We consume.
We are the world's greatest consumers—
eaters, drivers, users, buyers.
We earn money so we can
   have more
   build more
   use it
   throw it away
   buy more.
Is that why I'm working?
Is that why we have national economic problems?
Because we want more things
(whatever the cost)
and refuse to live simply?

No, Lord.
I don't want to be part of that.
Stiffen me against mindless consumption.
Keep my goals worthy
so that work is not just for money,
to have more things,
but for satisfaction and contribution—
giving rather than using.

The Privilege of Work

When I was young, my friend and I
would laugh with her mother, saying,
"Work, work, work!
That's all I ever do!"
It was a joke.
Now I am grateful for the privilege of work.
Whatever the task is,
there is a sense of being alive,
being needed,
when there is a job to do.
Whether I put away dried dishes,
type a letter,
or explain a difficult concept,
I have helped to keep order in our society,
I have loved someone by smoothing their path,
I have used myself for something other than
my own self-indulgence.
Work gives me a sense of worth.
Even though I know my true worth is inherent—
not the product of doing things,
but God's gift of simply being human—
still I thank you for meaningful work.

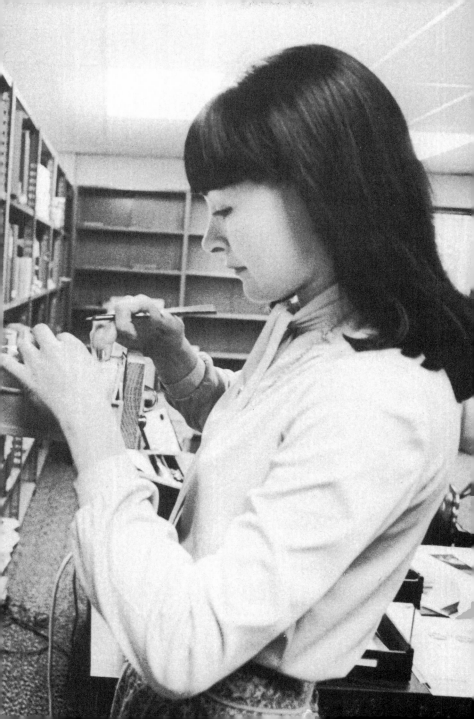

Leaving on a Trip

Lord, before we leave we ask your blessing.
We have planned
and I have saved my salary checks.
We have anticipated
    purchased
    packed.
Now we are ready to leave—
our whole family—
on a wonderful vacation
made possible by my working.
Thank you for this opportunity.
Help us to enjoy each other
and this uncluttered time together.
Teach us more of the world
and its people and natural beauty.
Guard our safety.
And, Lord, help us return
    refreshed
    changed
    better people.

Entertaining

Tonight we will be with close friends.
Our entertaining style is changed now
but we've gained something from it.

I used to fuss for company—
linens, flowers, fine food.
I still make an effort and a good meal
but I can't be quite as elaborate now.
Sometimes we simply have dessert
or cheeses and fruit.
There are times when I miss those extra touches,
but often I find we relax
and enjoy our friends more.
And we are more selective, Lord.
We entertain close friends for the most part.
Friendship has greater depth
because we think carefully
before extending an invitation.
We savor the opportunity to eat together,
to talk, to share more than trivialities.
We have learned to entertain
not out of obligation
nor with a sense of "putting on for show"
but with genuine loving hospitality.
Thank you for the lesson, Lord.

Another Woman's Criticism

It was a barbed remark—
a rusty cut at me.
She doesn't think I'm a "good" mother
because I work outside our home.
I feel both angry and defensive.

Different points of view are not easy to reconcile.
She cannot fully understand
   how my work energizes me
   how much happier a person I am
   how I enjoy my family more when I work.

Lord, help me not to make unfair judgments in return.
Her work is equally valuable—
salary does not determine worth.
She may feel slighted by unkind
or thoughtless comments
from people who demean the nonworking mother.
We both may tend to overlook
the satisfactions of each individual's choice.

I can and will forgive her
because I also make hasty and unfair remarks.
Help us talk more so that we better understand
our respective needs.

I Miss Volunteering

I miss volunteering, Lord.
Even though I sometimes resented
getting the uninteresting work
or the cast-off jobs of professionals,
I also miss the opportunities I had
for getting to know people
in the relaxed setting
of a church supper or a school library.
I don't have as much time to help as I did before.
I feel a little guilty
that I don't share the load
with other parents and church members.

Help me accept my limitations, Lord.
I can't do everything.
I need to set priorities.
I forget that I sometimes used to
fritter away time,
burning my candles at both ends,
busy with dozens of small jobs,
but lacking the feeling of meaningful contribution.
Help me accept that other people
can and do understand
when I must say no more often.
Give me your guidance
in a healthy conscience
and realistic self-expectations
that I might make good and helpful choices
about volunteering.

Somebody Help!

Lord, I need help
with dishes and beds and dusting,
with chauffeuring and washing.
I need support—
people around me to encourage me,
to back me up,
to lean on when I'm tired.
I need help.

Perhaps I haven't made my needs clear, Lord.
I think my family would give me help
if they understood
how and why I need it,
how I actually feel.
Perhaps I've relied on
whining or pleading
or the martyr malaise
rather than stating honestly
what my situation is.
People don't respect a "poor me" approach.

Help me, Lord,
to develop honest, fair ways of communication
so I don't have to complain,
feel sorry for myself,
or vainly try to be all things to all people.
Help, Lord.

Friendships Change

I spent an unusually long time
buying an anniversary gift
for old friends.
It's because we seldom see them anymore.
We haven't time.
Week nights I can't stay up late
and weekends are jammed with activities.
We've drifted apart.

I feel sad.
Yet friendships are constantly changing.
That in itself isn't bad—it's natural.
But, Lord, I am confronted with questions
as I shop for them today.
I have more money to spend
but I don't know as well
the people I spend it on.
Which relationships are most dear to me?
Were these people enjoyable acquaintances
or friends?
Do I miss their support or not?
Would I rather see such people more frequently
or continue in my work?
It isn't easy, Lord,
    adjusting to change
    evaluating relationships.
At least I don't take friendship
for granted anymore.
Help me continue to be a friend
in the real sense of the word
with those people with whom I can share
genuine love and support.
Help me determine what is most valuable in my life.

I Need Exercise

I sit too much these days.
I've grown accustomed to
   coffee breaks
   rolls
   treats.
It's not good for me.
For one thing, it's easy to gain weight
(and hard to lose it).
For another, I get weak.
My muscles aren't as firm
nor my limbs as flexible.
I tire more easily,
have less breathing capacity.
I need exercise.
My mind and brain are busy
but they'd feel better
if the rest of me was moving too.
I can relax work tensions better when I
   take a brisk walk
   bike to the store
   walk instead of taking the elevator
   simply stretch now and then.
I miss my weekly volleyball or tennis.
Perhaps I'm doing myself a disservice.
You intend that all of me be healthy.
I will try to take better care of myself
and exercise,
starting today.
Help me keep at it, Lord.

Mornings

Mornings can be chaotic!
There are so many people
and schedules
and notes to teachers,
a preschooler to bundle,
lunches, lost belts, books,
breakfasts, and buses to catch.
All this, and only one bathroom!
How do we do it, five days a week?

I must say,
we do it rather well!
It's not always smooth or friendly
(not everyone "likes" morning)
But we get everyone off on time
    the dishes cleared if not cleaned
    lunches in hand
    and have time to make beds.
I feel proud, Lord,
that we are able to successfully
    divide duties
    manage our individual caretaking
    move into a fresh day, prepared.
Thank you for our ability
to do this each morning.

Sick Day

Sick!
I haven't *time* to be sick.
I have a job to do—
two jobs.
I can't spend my time in bed
   nursing a terrible cold
   coughing
   sleeping!
I have work to do.

Yes, Lord,
I do have work to do.
There will always be work to do.
But calm me down.
I need to be healthy
   strong
   rested
   well fed
in order to do my work.
Lord, I lose track of my personal care
in my striving to do my jobs.
Perhaps this ugly cold
is a lesson for me.
I need to do a better job
of taking care of myself.
Now, with your blessing,
I shall rest and heal.

The Male-Dominated Work World

We change slowly, Lord.
At times we change almost imperceptibly
and we resist change subtly.
But I feel a resistance
against me.
Men expect me to prove myself—
   not to miss work (they sometimes do)
   to show I can achieve
   to maintain both jobs in superior form
   to accept lower pay
      because I am predicted to be
      less faithful, less dependable.
If I hold back,
I'm a "dependent female."
If I suggest a change,
I'm "too aggressive."
I get mad!

I'm a person.
I work hard.
I am not "all women"—
I'm me.
I look for a day when we will see
that different individuals
can contribute to all areas.
An organized man
can manage household tasks,
and a logical woman
can balance books.
A sensitive man

can work in personnel or child care.
A kind and capable woman
can manage a group of workers
or a hospital section.
I look for a time
when we are all encouraged
rather than measured or judged.
"There is neither Jew nor Greek, . . .
    slave nor free, . . .
    male nor female."
Give me patience without overcompensation
and take away my own biases.

Repetition and Teaching

Fall.
Cool autumn.
This was always the season for reminding.
  "Close the door!"
  "Did you close the door?"
Repetition teaches children—
reminding over and over,
"Close the door!"
I'm not home after school to do that anymore.
I wonder if it's getting closed?
Is it important, Lord?
I remember how I used to find myself harping—
even nagging.
Small things used to bother me more
  open doors
  crumbs left on the counter
  dirty socks on the bedroom floor.
I don't have time for nagging like I used to.
In fact, I have only time to say things
in a teaching way:
  "We all need to keep the house
  in order, because we haven't time
  to pick up over and over."
I say it once and let others bear the results
if the socks don't get washed.
Perhaps I'm discovering a new set of priorities
as I'm working—
learning what is really important
and what is secondary for a smooth-running household.
Lord, maybe I'm a better mother and teacher—
less a nag.

Sunday Morning Worship

Lord, I'd love to sleep in on Sunday.
Day after day I'm up and going
   work
   Saturday chores
   family activities.
Sunday morning,
and a rainy one at that,
would be such a good time to sleep late.

Give me a nudge, Lord.
The children need my example
if they are to develop worship habits.
I can choose to sleep Saturday
rather than Sunday—
the chores will wait.
And once I put my feet on the floor
I'll be all right.
The service will both inspire and relax me.
I can get out of myself
   my schedule
   my tasks
and think about what life is,
what it means to be a creature in your world.
You're right, Lord,
   I need to get going.
   I need worship.
   I need you.
I'll nap later.

Dealing with Pressure

Lord, sometimes I don't cope well.
The pressures of the work world
press down on me until my neck aches
or my head feels thick and groggy.
Working in this Western culture
which derives satisfaction (and profit)
from increasing productivity
   quick thinking
   competition
can be very taxing,
even alien,
to the human spirit and body.

Still, I can learn to cope.
Help me, Lord,
to be patient with myself
and realistic about my limitations.
Help me learn to intentionally relax.
Help me create a physical and
mental environment at work
where I can shut out external pressures
in a moment of meditation.
Give me a far-reaching vision which allows me
   to take one day at a time
   to keep things in perspective
   to trust you and life
   to cope with pressure.

Personality Conflicts

I have a personality conflict problem at work, Lord,
and you're the only one I can talk to.
I can't tell my boss yet
because I need to think things over.
If I talk among coworkers
I may be viewed as gossiping or complaining.
My family doesn't really understand—
    they listen
    they sympathize
but they can't know the situation
and don't dare advise me.

Help me weigh things, Lord.
What do I do to antagonize?
    to promote good will?
    to help?
    to encourage?
When do I unnecessarily compete?
When do I make hasty judgments?
When do I withhold my honest opinion
for the sake of peace?
If I can come to a good understanding
of my personality and behavior
and the motivations or difficulties of another
then I may be able to talk with someone else
or change my behavior.
Until then, Lord, thanks for listening
and for your guidance.

Office Pettiness

People can be petty;
especially people who work together
day after day
and who may have little else in common.
I get tired of snide remarks
   gossip
   small complaints.
Bickering wears down my cheerfulness
and comparing is often wasted energy.

Give me the strength I need
to rise above pettiness.
I don't want to act haughty or self-righteous—
"holier-than-they"—
nor do I want to get snared
in a web of sticky inferences
and personnel politics.
It isn't easy, because I have my own
priorities, ambitions, and opinions
which color my attitudes.
I don't always see the best in everyone.

Keep me on a straight path, Lord—
keep me hardworking, caring, honest
and, with your help,
modeling your integrity.

Warmed by Praise

It means a lot to me
to receive praise for a job well done.
When my boss complimented me
my smile flourished
and I was richly warmed inside.
We need praise.
You knew that, Lord,
as you called to attention
those who loved and served you well.

Now that I am basking in satisfaction,
help me to extend the blessing to others
   to notice what the children
     did *right* today
   to send a note of thanks
   to give my husband a kiss.
Just as I welcome praise
let me share its warmth.

Fringe Benefits

The world is full of interesting things!
Lunch hour today found me
with a French couple,
   intelligent
   friendly
   eager to learn
     about our country
     and its businesses.
I was the fortunate one—
   hearing them describe their customs
   learning about their work
   welcomed by their kindness.
And tomorrow they'll come to dinner
at our house
where my whole family can meet them!
Thank you for another opportunity,
a benefit of my working.
Lead me to use and appreciate these
opportunities to their fullest.

Friends at Work

It took some time
but now I have friends at work.
We're finally past that stage of
"How are you, fine"
and "I'm so far behind this week!"
We talk about real things
   our feelings about people
   our concerns about work
   our struggles
   our personal joys.
As I hear about these people's lives
I understand them better.
I feel much more sympathetic,
patient, or helpful
when I actually know the person
I'm working with—
know them "inside."
A secretary becomes a woman,
a vice-president, a father.
I have a chance to be myself among others,
to discover that I have gifts to give them—
understanding, empathy, a "tip,"
or a new joke just for fun.
I appreciate this opportunity to get to know
more of the people of your world.
Thank you, Lord.

Time to Think

One thing I miss with working
is the time to think—alone.
After the children got off to school,
I used to be able to spend time alone.
I would dust
and debate internal conflicts.
I would scrub
and consider what I wanted to clean up
in my relationships.
I had time to read—
and how I loved it!—
   a good novel
   a new writer
   a probing book about politics.

I think one of the values
of working in the home
is that one can come to know oneself.
I was able to spend time
   pondering my meaning
   examining my values
   thinking about the future
   sorting out feelings, relationships.

Now I am much busier
and I forget to think quietly.
I shall have to take a look at my schedule
and build in some time
for thinking about the meaning of life.
I am here for a reason, Lord.
I want to understand and experience life.
Help me not to be so busy "experiencing"
that I forget to understand.

Looking Back

I have changed since I went to work.
I was the one who had been happy at home.
I still am.
I like my family, my home.
But I have added something to my life.
Confidence.
I have tried more new experiences
during my first months of working
than I had tried for years previous.
I had to travel alone.
I learned to get around in unfamiliar areas.
I developed skill in organization.
I became more quickly sensitive to my children
   their health
   their quietness
   their disappointments
because I needed to be perceptive.
I didn't have time to wait to be told.
I am less self-centered.
I appreciate friends and people who help me.
I am grateful for the surge of pleasure,
the pride that comes when someone says
I have accomplished a task at work.

These experiences can't be taken away
whether I work for years or only for another week.
I have grown because I have dared to try,
dared to fail,
and I made it!
I altered my life pattern and made it!
Thank you, Lord, for giving me this opportunity
to learn more about myself.

Am I Too Aggressive?

There has been a feeling for years
that a woman among men—
a career woman—
will become aggressive,
like men.
Thank you, Lord, for the magazine
that helped me set that straight.

I have changed.
I am assertive now,
more than I was before I worked.
Assertive is not aggressive.
Aggressive can be unpleasant,
   nasty at times
   insensitive
   a "steam roller" approach.
I have not learned to be aggressive
and men are not necessarily aggressive either—
it depends on the person.

But I have learned to be assertive.
I can state my point of view
   express anger in manageable ways
   tell someone my opinion
   feel successful without destroying.
I can be assertive without ignoring others.
In fact, I think I am more honest now.
I'm not afraid to express my feelings
so they tend not to get buried

where they can sneak out in other ways
which hurt people.
I am more sensitive
because I have to think before I speak.
I do not allow people to use me,
to hurt me or treat me badly.
That's being assertive too.
It has nothing to do with my sex, Lord.
I am still a woman
and a person.
It's just that now I am proud of being me
and unafraid to be honest
about how I really feel.
It is a great gain.

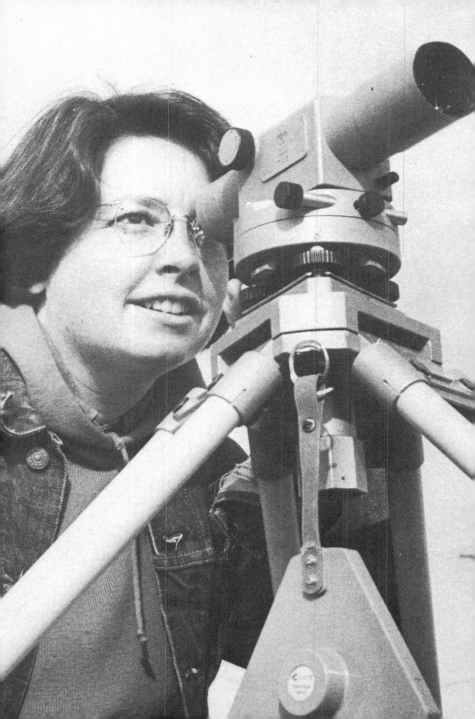

Fulfillment

I could have worked another three hours.
Not only because I had so much to do
but because I enjoy it.
It's a good thing to like work—
to see it less as duty,
more as contribution.
This is more than self-satisfaction, Lord.
This is a sense of
  being what I'm intended to be
  giving
  fulfilling my destiny
  growing.
It's not something I take lightly.
I am in touch with life
in its best sense
when I am fulfilling my capabilities
for the benefit of your world.
Thank you, Lord, for my work.

I Want a Raise

I'd like to pray for a raise, Lord.
We could really use it.
It would be nice to be rewarded for good work.

I struggle with my desire for more earnings
and my awareness of how I use them—
my stewardship of my earnings.
Am I seeking reward
   to be used for significant things
   to be shared with the church
   to be a blessing to someone
or am I seeking earnings to buy more things
   which will succumb to obsolescence
   which are merely symbols of power
   which are only objects of entertainment?
Why do I want more money?

Help me, Lord,
to value money for more than itself,
to see the mission of money—
   the goodness it can provide
   the people it can help.
Create a spirit of openness in me
so I understand that money is only
a means to providing happiness—
it will not bring me happiness
unless I give it meaningful tasks.
Make me content with what I have, if need be,
able to let go of the need to possess,
willing to share and give
as you have so willingly given to me.

Changing the System

There are traditions which are hard to challenge.
There are people who are in power.
There are thoughts and concepts
which are not easily questioned.
I feel like a small person
in a rigid structure.
I feel powerless to change the system.

Perhaps my problem is patience.
Things do not get rearranged or rethought
overnight, or even in a year.
People need evidence
   time to consider
   trust in the person who suggests change.
I may have to wait awhile.

I may also have to realign my expectations.
Systems are not always flexible,
institutions often strangle human considerations.
I must weigh what it is possible to change
and how to work within the system
in order to affect change through other people.
Then, if I cannot make my mark,
I have the opportunity to leave
or to accept what I can't change.
Is the principle most important
or can I adjust when the system doesn't change?
Help me decide, Lord.

Facing My Boss

I dread bringing my problem to my supervisor.
I think nearly everyone is in awe
of the person in power,
whether that person is a "dragon"
or an understanding leader.

I have to talk to myself,
get my feelings straight.
I am as much a worthy person
as those people in charge of my work.
I have a valid concern to discuss
and I am prepared for the meeting.
I am able to be pleasant and clear.

Help me, Lord.
Sit with me in that office for those
few moments.
Keep my head clear and my mouth not so dry.
Let me trust my ability
so that I say what I mean.
Release me from self-doubt
and turn me over to trust
so that I can expect the best outcome
from this tense situation.
Remind me that the real power is in you,
whatever happens in the office.

Pride in My Appearance

I should always respect myself enough
to take care how I look.
But I often let my appearance lag when I was home.
It was easy to forget to brush my hair
   polish my nails
   straighten my clothes.
Jeans and tennis shoes were the rule
and occasionally I'd slop around in slippers
nearly all day.

I have to be more careful now.
I haven't time for fingernail polish
and it often gets marred anyway,
but I do have to appear more tidy.
I like it.
I like taking time for myself—
   repairing a small seam opening
   checking my eyebrow line, my lipstick.
I feel good about myself when I am
neatly dressed, looking fresh.

I don't think it's vanity, Lord.
It's pride, in its best sense.
I want to be all I am able to be—
my best self.
My job helps me build a sense of
wholeness about myself,
a desire to be fully alive.
I appreciate the change in me.
I need not have been careless before
(I would not return to that)
but I'm glad that my job has brought me
this new personal awareness.

School Events

It's hard for me to miss school events.
My daughter is very excited about her concert;
she will be playing cello.
I hate to miss it.
My son is participating in field day
and I'd like to watch him run.

This is one of the sacrifices I must make
if I am going to work.
I notice that the children of my friend
don't expect her to come—
she also works.
They understand that she is occupied,
but she has also let them know they achieve
whether or not they have an audience.
Perhaps that lesson is more important.

Perhaps I can find times
when I can support their efforts in other ways.
I will surely want to hear all about the events
when we share news at dinnertime.
I can have someone tape the concert,
or listen to their practicing
which is also important.
I can remember that I share many other events
with my children—
our relationship doesn't rest on a racing effort.

Bless my children, Lord,
as they grow and participate in life
whether or not I am there to see the "show."
Their opportunity to try is the greater gain.

Continuing Education

I can earn more with a degree.
It seems simple—
  go back to school
  finish that degree.
But it's not simple at all.
How in the world can I manage more?
There are so many demands on my energy already.
I would have to give up something—
  a measure of neatness at home
  time with my family
  entertainment, community activities.
Is it worth it?

On the other hand, I may work for a long time.
A degree will boost me,
not only in salary
but in self-esteem and job responsibility.
I am capable of learning.
I discovered that when I started this job.
"Old dogs" learn "new tricks" better than
young puppies after all.
We've got the experience to aid learning.
Perhaps I can relinquish something else for awhile.

Another decision.
But life is made to be lived
and decisions are ultimately adventures.
Help me reason this one out, Lord.
Whatever choice I make, I will be learning.

Before Children

I was thinking back to the "B.C." days—
"before children."
When we first knew we would have a child
how wonderful it was!
We were on the edge of an opportunity
to know, watch, and nurture
a person,
a whole new person.
In a mysterious way
we felt privileged and challenged.
We were thrilled!—
and scared.
A person, a child, would need us
    learn from us
    come to know life through us.
A miraculous mystery
of enormous consequence
which I sometimes forget
because I am so busy
taking care of my family.

Lord, help me remember
as I work for my children and help them
and grow impatient or tired—
these are those mysterious promises
we once awaited in awe.
Bless my children.
Please help me see life with them as a gift
    to cherish
    to handle carefully (for they can be fragile)
and for which I give you
my thanks.

The Big Cleanup

At last!
We have found a way to manage housecleaning.
Thank you, Lord, for the inspiration!

Thursday night is the family's night to clean.
Everyone has a job to do
and an area to be responsible for.
It took a little hounding at first
(forgive my impatience)
but eventually we developed an operation
which includes everyone and gets the job done!

The net gain is more than organized cleaning—
although the satisfaction of a neat home
is rewarding to every person.
The side benefits are that we are together
    we are cooperating
    we share achievement
    we are more efficient, less complaining
    we even laugh at ourselves
    (what else can we do when Dad
    tips over the scrub pail?).
Thanks for the willingness of my family
to give this system a try.
We feel good about this family project
and about discovering it together.

New Understanding

I used to be piqued by the common situation
of people dividing themselves at parties;
men and a few women talked business,
the rest of the women talked home and family.
I didn't think there was much growing going on—
few people learned to appreciate
the point of view or struggle of others.
Worse, there was an unspoken message which said
home and family talk was of less value
than business talk.
I resented that.

I used to imagine that the business world
was not only exciting, but easier to deal with
than the world of home and family.
Somehow I dreamed that my husband went to work,
did his job which was challenging and interesting,
and left, unruffled, unperturbed.
Now I see better.

Both worlds of work are rewarding and frustrating.
I understand my husband's life more now—
his ups and downs, the occasional boredom,
the problems and challenges.
He also understands what it means to
raise a family, keep a home, manage a household.

It's too bad, Lord, that we feel a need to compete,
to rank jobs, life-styles.
All of us have common needs and satisfactions.
I hope we will share more of them among ourselves
so that we respect the work of each, of all.
Help us hear and help us share.

Taking Advantage of Me

Someone isn't carrying a fair share of the load
and I'm left to pick up the excess.
I resent it.
I have enough to do in my busy life
without having to fill in for someone else.
I feel angry.

What shall I do about it?
I feel shy about speaking to a supervisor—
like the kids used to say,
"Tattle-tale!"
Yet I know I can't continue to carry for two,
not without hurting my job
or my family and me.

First, I have to ask myself some questions.
Am I choosing to carry double?
Do I pick up a load because I feel responsible
that things go right at any cost?
Am I taking on someone else's problem
because I am not comfortable with imperfection?
If I let go, will the logical consequences be
that the other person will have to change?
Do I feel a heightened sense of importance
at being the "good guy," the martyr?
Am I covering for another
because I feel sorry for that person,

unable to help them in any other way?
Am I afraid to confront the person
because I hate conflict, even mild conflict?

My reasons for helping may be faulty.
My choosing to help may not be helpful to anyone;
the company or the person.
Lord, lead me to a way of solving this situation.
I may need to inform someone in supervision.
I may need to confront the person who is
taking advantage of me.
One thing is sure,
something has to change.
I'll need your help to start, Lord.
Help me be fair and kind, but firm.

A Chance for Promotion

I am at once thrilled and confused.
I have a chance for an excellent promotion
   a good job with higher salary
   an opportunity to move east
   a chance to try an exciting field
and I don't know what to do.
Help me, Lord, to sort it out.

My family.
Will a move disrupt their lives too much?
It will mean new schools, friends, surroundings.
How will my husband feel about leaving his job?
Competitive or encouraging of me?
Myself.
Do I want to change now or shall I wait?
Is this a singular opportunity,
something that may not come again?
Is my job the primary force in our lives?
Am I weighing all sides fairly?
My employer.
Will I let them down by not taking the job?
Do they prefer to keep me in my present position?
Can I handle the increased responsibility?

There is so much to consider.
I must take more time, talk to more people.
Give me patience and steadiness, Lord.
I will look for your direction
   in the words of friends and coworkers,
   in the feelings of my family
   in my truest heart, my honest self.
I feel overwhelmed, excited, and challenged.
Help me make the best possible decision.

I'm Bored

Bored! Bored! Bored!
I am tired of my routine at work
and I can't seem to get any life into it.
I am on a moving sidewalk—
standing still but carried along
by the motion of the sidewalk
going down some tunnel and arriving nowhere.
Bored.

Is it me? The season, the demands of home?
Is it the job? The repetition, the people?
Is it a lack of meaning
   a job which has no future
   no sense of contributing to the world,
   just "something to do," that's all?

Help me sort it out.
Being bored is worse than being tired.
I need to be energized
if not by taking on a new task
(people might appreciate my initiative)
then by finding other outlets for my creativity
away from work.
I must do *something* to relieve the feeling
of soggy blankets over my head.
Read some jokes, call a friend,
take an honest look at my job
and my capabilities.
What shall I change and when shall I begin?
Begin now by stretching
my body and my thoughts.
With your help
I can break free from this boredom.

Handling Stress

There are days when pressure leans on me
like straight winds of 50 miles an hour.
My neck tires
   the lower back of my head throbs
   my shoulders ache
   I long for relief.

Some of the stress is inevitable—
   a deadline must be met
   an appointment must be kept.
Some of it is self-induced by unnecessary worry
or my misguided attitude that
to be burdened is to be important.

I can find ways to deal with stress.
Occasionally I need to take time
to get away from my source of stress
and relax,
even if it's just a walk around the block
or a rest in the lounge.
I can slough off unhealthy attitudes
which drive me towards unproductive overwork.
I can run or play tennis or take vigorous walks
when my body yearns to release tension.

And, finally, I can take some moments
to focus in on my life's meaning
   on beauty around me
   on the goodness of God and loving people.
Moments to concentrate on deeper thoughts
which can peel away the external pressures
and expose the meaning of life.

I Need Confidence

It's going to be a tough assignment.
I am having pangs of inadequacy
   a jittery stomach
   a distracted mind
   loss of sleep.
Can I do the job?
Will I fail?

Help me concentrate, Lord—
concentrate on the job
and on accomplishing
rather than fearing failure.
Help me grab hold of my abilities
   trust myself
   recognize that I can achieve.
Help me remember that I was hired
because people believed in me.
Everyone goes through these moments.
It's a sign that I care about my work
and it's a challenge to try.
Failure isn't the end of the world
and satisfaction in doing my best
is worth the effort.
Stay with me, Lord,
and we'll go at this together!

Best Friends

When we met for coffee, I knew we had changed.
I am working outside the home,
she is not.
There is a mild tension,
a new distance, between us.
We haven't the same news to share,
she doesn't know my "territory,"
my coworkers.
I want to be close,
but sometimes I can't adequately tell her
how happy I am, how good I feel.
We are drifting apart
and both of us hurt from it.

How do we learn to live in changing relationships?
Do we acknowledge that life is full of change
or do we try to keep friendships fresh?
Is it realistic to think I will see her
often enough to maintain our former closeness?

Help me, Lord,
not to exclude my friend from my life.
Help me also to accept the separation feelings
I am now experiencing.
Perhaps we need to talk openly about what's happening
for certainly we both feel it.
Yes, if we can talk about it
the tension will be lessened
and perhaps the friendship will grow.
Be with us, Lord,
as we risk being honest.

A Mistake

I made an error
and it was costly.
My company will have to recover a loss
because I wasn't accurate.
I feel humiliated.

Lord, help me forgive myself.
Sometimes I play God
and punish myself
far more than you would.
I forget that you have forgiven me.
I worry about what the others are thinking.
Will they trust me again?
Do they regret hiring me?
Am I a fool in someone's eyes?

Give me perspective, Lord.
I have performed capably.
This is one of few mistakes.
The company won't suffer great loss.
And people have given me no reason to believe
that they reject me.
In fact, because I was quick
to discover my error and admit it,
they were very considerate.
I am caught up in my own need to be in charge.
I hate to admit weakness
and I overcompensate for that truth
by not forgiving myself.
Nobody's perfect.
That's what Jesus was all about.
Help me forgive myself.

Child-Care Center

It's not easy to find a good child-care center.
I'm grateful our church provides one.
And it isn't easy leaving my small ones
in the care of others.
Sometimes I feel guilty
or I wonder if I'm missing something
    a first experience
    a happy moment
    a needed hug.
Today my youngest child burst from the classroom
all smiles,
a finger painting in hand.
I never took time to teach our first child
how to finger paint.
I didn't always "tune in."
I missed some first experiences,
even when I was right in the next room.

Children can find new discoveries
special learnings, friends,
independence, and warm, patient care
in the stimulating atmosphere
of a good child-care center or at home.
Today the most important things I did
were to listen to my child
describe that colorful painting
and open my arms for a hug.
A child can be loved by many people
    in different ways
    in different settings.
It is the quality of the time I give,
not the number of hours I'm nearby,
which will develop our relationship.

Crisis Mentality

"The tail wags the dog."
That's the truth for me lately!
Some seasons are worse than others
and some children need more time.
Right now I live from crisis to crisis
just trying to get everything done
and barely able to think ahead.

Although I know this can happen in any life,
help me, Lord, to live more intentionally.
I have learned the hard way—
having no goals means I arrive someplace
but it may not be where I would have hoped.
Not to plan
is to plan to live in confusion.
Not to dream and tie the dreams down
is like a nightmare—
running, chasing, wishing,
scattered thoughts and energies,
people making demands which I follow unthinkingly.

I am an organized person in some ways,
but I need to have more direction in my life.
I can make clear goals for short periods of time.
I'll start with a week,
set a measurable goal, perhaps two—
some tasks I know I can achieve
and which I can see I accomplished.
Then, when other things try to interfere,

I can consciously decide to change my goal
or fulfill it and reevaluate the other need.
At least I won't be aimlessly going about
meeting deadlines I detest
or demands which exclude my needs.
I'll have to write them down
    check them off
    put the list where I can see it.
I'll certainly have to begin *right now*
    before the phone rings
    before the children have another request.
My first goal—
to set goals for tomorrow
and perhaps for this week.
Goals I can achieve.
Just starting will help ease the pressure.
I don't have to live in a crisis mentality.
I can choose to change.

Time for Myself

The person who gets the least amount
of my time these days
is me.
I don't read,
I don't muse,
I don't walk.
I'm on a treadmill.

This is not what you intend, Lord.
I am not enriched,
not growing or giving,
when I sacrifice my own renewal
on an altar of "should do" tasks.

Help me face this realistically
and fairly.
One benefit of working is
doing something I enjoy—self-fulfillment.
One detriment is lack of private time.
Help me snatch moments—
   breathe quiet as I water the garden
      at twilight
   empty my mind on the way home from work
   walk rather than drive when possible
   attend a weekend church retreat.
I do not choose to be selfish, Lord.
But I do welcome and value moments of renewal.
Thank you for your support
and for quiet moments.

A Child in Trouble

My child is having problems.
I can't sort out my responsibility.
On the one hand, I feel I might have prevented this.
Perhaps if I'd been home after school?
Was there something I neglected to teach?
Did I not listen because I was overtired?
Does my working upset his equilibrium?
On the other hand, I must also ask:
Would he have made the same choice
whether or not I were present?
Is this a situation children often face
whether or not a mother works?
Am I magnifying the problem,
complicating it with self-doubt?

Sometimes there are no easy answers.
Lord, I need some good, honest friends
and perhaps some wise advice.
I need to stand back a bit
    try to be less emotional
    trust the people who can offer help.
One problem is not the end of the world,
nor can it be brushed aside.
Help me keep a sense of balance,
aware that Jesus showed us the way—
forgiveness, understanding, patience,
love, and firmness are in the right.
Help me be an understanding parent,
honest with myself about my responsibilities,
loving toward my child who needs my guidance.

Freedom to Choose

We sometimes let ourselves be locked in by decisions.
Rather than saying
    I was wrong
    I need to reconsider
we drive on relentlessly—
    I have to
    I must.
Only when our bodies are exhausted
or our spirits drained
do we consider rest or change.

Now that I've decided to work at this job,
give me the wisdom to not be driven mindlessly.
Whether or not to work is often a choice,
and even when it's a necessity,
where and how I work remains my choice.
There is freedom in knowing I can change.
I can always review priorities of
    money
    time
    self-interest
    others.
I'm not locked in unless I choose to be
either by refusing to change
or by resisting a situation I cannot change.
No situation in life is permanent.
Guide my choices, Lord.

What Is Self-Interest?

Working has refined my theology.
I've learned to act on my own behalf.
Somewhere I got the idea
that self-interest means selfish.
It doesn't.
Thank goodness!
Self-interest is taking care of myself.
I take care of my body, which sustains me.
I also take care of my spirit—
that part of me that needs love
in order to survive.
I must be nourished to stay alive.
I must ask people—
my family, friends, coworkers—
to treat me kindly
just as I want to treat them.
If I don't ask, they may not know what I need.
I can tell when my spirit and body are underfed—
    it's when I want to cry, but don't
    when I'm angry and say nothing
    when I want to be touched
    when I need sleep.
I'm feeling undernourished
    when I resent the demands of others
    when I long for praise
    when I play games in order to get attention.

Self-interest is asking for what I need and want
    not at the expense of others
    nor at my whim

but because God expects me
to take good care of myself,
my valuable life.
I ask the world's people
to love me and help care for me
because I know
God wants me to be well fed.

Weather

Why do I resist weather?
It's a useless waste of energy!
Still, snow and cold are inconvenient
when I'm trying to get to work on time.
Spring rains bring muddy kitchen floors
and worse, muddy carpets!
My greatest bout is with clouds—
depressing, sleepy weather.

I need to adjust my attitude.
I can't change the weather, that's for sure!
Better that I should use my energies
to find a sunny friend on a cloudy day
or to share rides on buses or in car pools
when I tire of snow and cold.
I can appreciate the crisp freshness of cold air.
Spring rains bring green grass
and flowers in all that dirt.
Resisting weather
is resisting reality
and it's a futile human attempt
to control the world.
Help me, Lord,
to accept my place as a human being
rather than foolishly resisting and complaining.
I need my energy for other things.

Rules

Oh! how I wish there were simple rules!
If only every child were the same
   same needs and strengths
   same conflicts and pressures
so that one rule would fit all.
But it isn't so.
One child needs more limits,
another is crushed by the same.
One person makes good decisions,
the next needs advice,
and the next is reluctant
or brazenly independent.
"Never" becomes impossible
and "right" needs qualification.

Help me get beyond codes and rules.
Jesus knew it wasn't enough—
his church had codified so many things
it lost a sense of awareness
for what was meaningful.
Jesus lived and underscored
overall attitudes necessary to life—
to seek loving understanding
   respectful acceptance
   meaningful restraint.

Help me be open to each child,
   forgiving
   trying to empathize
   guiding more than guarding
and living out your spirit
as much as or more than the law.

Too Tired to Cook

There are days when I dread dinner.
I'm just too tired to cook.
When I get into the house
I want to rest, not cook.
But my family (and I) are hungry.
We need food.

Help me be creative, Lord.
Part of my attitude is physical weariness.
A five-minute rest
and a glass of juice might perk me up.
Part of this feeling comes from trying to be
"Super-Mom."
Other family members can help
since they also need to eat.
I can solve my dilemma thoughtfully.
Sometimes it pays to eat out.
Often I can plan ahead so I have
at least one "ready-reserve" meal on hand.
Of course I'm tired at the end of the day,
but with your help
and some planning
I can make a meal and enjoy it with my family.

My Husband

When it comes to dividing time among family members
the children often get more than my husband.
It's so easy to let it happen—
they are the ones who need transportation
   help with homework
   a listener
   a cook
   a bike mechanic.
There I am again,
   struggling to keep my head above water
   drowning in tasks
   virtually too tired to talk to my husband.

The only way we can keep our relationship alive
is to get away from the others.
We go out for coffee or supper
or just for a walk in the neighborhood.
It is a time we can have to unwind
to try to share a bit of our day
and especially to say something meaningful
about how that day affected us:
   "I feel caught by my current deadline"
   "I missed you when you had to skip lunch"
   "I'm proud of how you handled the children"
   "I'm disappointed we can't go away."
Lord, it's hard work to maintain a relationship

when the activities around us are so many.
It's hard to avoid talking about schedules
and focus in on personal meanings—
how we feel about what we're doing.

Dedicate me to this relationship.
Long ago I chose to know and understand this person.
I still don't know all of him
and I can continue to enjoy discovering
how he changes.
I can learn from him
if I take time for him.
Help me remember to take time for my husband.

The Seventh Commandment

Someone's stealing pencils again
and small, supposedly unnoticed, items—
a stapler here, tape there.
We rationalize that nobody will miss it
or that we "deserve" some fringe benefits.
The truth is we're stealing
and somebody has to pay the bill.
Ultimately it is we who indirectly pay
because the company can't afford
as big a raise as we might like.
And our spirits pay more dearly—
it takes energy to rationalize our actions.
Small chinks in our moral codes
are not easily replaced,
and are more easily enlarged.
Help me, Lord,
not to be inflexibly super-righteous,
but to remain honest with my employer
and especially with myself.

Competition

I am experiencing more competition
now that I'm working.
People compare themselves to each other.
I used to do it too, with
   hot dish recipes
   housecleaning techniques
   my list of volunteer credits.
Somehow it seems worse now,
probably because there are financial rewards
for superior performance.
People are prone to compete vigorously
for financial reward.

Help me keep my life balanced.
I am a competitive person.
In fact, it helps me achieve
and I would not cast it out of my life completely.
I would, Lord, place my competitiveness
against a background of caring for others
and taking care of myself.
I would take care of my sense of moral values,
my self-respect.
I would care for the people I work with
rather than compete for their attention
or excel them at any cost.
I would remain true to the principles
I have learned, accepted,
and now have a chance to demonstrate
as I live with the reality of competition.
I would keep my Christian values
at the top of my list.

Quitting a Job

This is a terrible decision!
I want to change jobs—
certainly I want to quit this job.
I am not suited to it any longer.
I am not doing my best work
because I am unhappy.
But I stay because I don't know how to quit.

I will be able to get through this
if I give it good thought.
First I can list the hazards and the advantages
of quitting.
Next I can begin to search for other jobs
before I quit here
to give me some sense of security.
I can ask people for advice
and consider the long-term effects
of leaving and staying.
Then I can write it all out if necessary—
   what I need and want
   what I might say to my supervisor.
Then I will be ready to take the plunge
into new water, a fresh start.

Lord, I get tangled up in thinking
that any decision is forever.
You have told me again and again
that life is full of new starts.
I can always return to a former vocation—
if not in this office setting,

in another like it.
I might find great satisfaction
and new challenges if I change.
Quitting isn't necessarily desertion—
it may be an opportunity to grow!
Even if I make a poor decision, a bad choice,
I can learn from it.
Help me by giving me courage
   to change
   to quit
   to begin again
to dare to learn
by doing.
I will sleep better once I make the choice.
Help me, Lord.

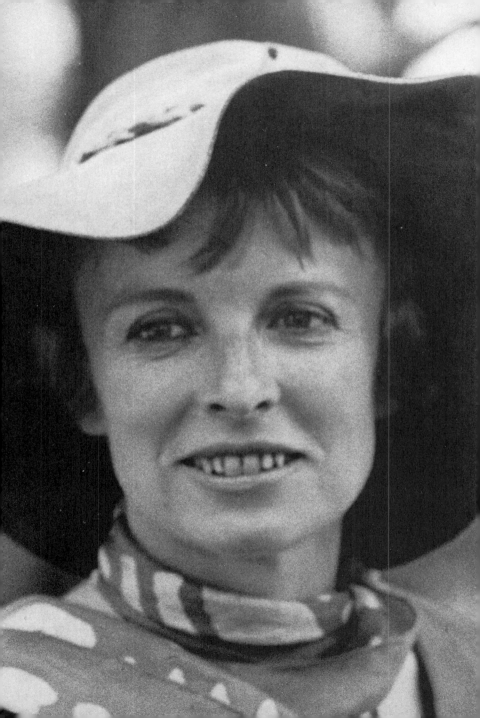

New Horizons

There's a whole world out here that I've missed.
Some of it is very exciting!
People from all over the world
live and work around me.
People with different ideas
    customs
    experiences.
Life sparkles more now that I've met them—
there is so much to learn and share!
Many of them can teach me much about life.

Then there are people and experiences
which confront me.
People with values which contradict mine.
Situations which are painful,
which remind me of the poverty life contains—
    poverty of possessions and wants,
    poverty of spirits and souls.
I see more pain than I used to see.

Lord, whether I see difficulty, pain,
and meaninglessness in lives
or I experience joy and gratitude
as I enjoy people and situations—
whatever I meet in this vast world of yours—
help me hang on to the hope that you offer.
I can always believe in life—
whatever it holds for me,
however it takes shape in the people around me.
I need not cast aside life

because I experience differences or pain.
I can welcome whatever I meet
because you strengthen me, love me,
and seek to have me understand my purpose.
I am confronted
not so that I might judge and cast away,
but so that I can love and build up
in your name.

Afraid of Leisure

One of the hazards of working
is that I get so scheduled,
so involved in activity,
that I don't know how to relax.
I begin to feel guilty
if I'm sitting still.
I look about, frantically,
for something to do
anytime I have a spare moment.

I wonder if I'm losing my ability
to enjoy life,
an unstructured, open life
when things can happen spontaneously
and be enjoyed for their mere happening?
Have I watched the sun rise or set lately?
Have I laughed at a firefly
or wished on a star?
Have I taken time to pray,
to wonder about why I was born,
or who might need to be sung to?
Have I listened to the birds,
or smiled at the children
playing with ants on the sidewalk?
Am I too busy, Lord,
to live?

A Juggler

Six balls in the air
  job
  family
  housework
  church
  community
  recreation
Every day I juggle these balls
and often I wonder,
"Which one can I let drop today?"
Many times I scold myself
as I let one or another bounce
for a day, a week.
Most often I drop recreation
  my own growing
  my rest
  my learning.
I feel more guilty if I drop any of the others.

I need to change my attitude,
not notice so much which ball I drop for awhile.
Rather I could consider and feel proud—
with all the balls I juggle,
think of how many
I successfully keep in the air!

Thanks for the strength to do all I do.